PRAISE FOR
FROM THREE HEARTBEATS TO ONE

Keisha Wells transforms her unimaginable experience of loss and grief into an irreplaceable tool for those who have also suffered the loss of a child. *From Three Heartbeats to One* is undeniably an exceptional resource. This book provides the love, understanding, and support needed for the thousands of families that face this devastating loss.

Shannon Pittman Duraso
Volunteer Leader for March of Dimes

Keisha is truly using her pain for purpose by sharing her loss story in *From Three Heartbeats to One*. Not only is she giving you practical tools but she is sharing real life examples of how to remove the shame and stigma associated with pregnancy and infant loss. I love the work Keisha is doing and know you will be blessed by her work.

Erica M. McAfee
Founder of Sisters in Loss

Keisha Wells takes readers on a candid journey through the healing process of grief and loss. Keisha compassionately removes the veil of doom and gloom, and shines light on the ability to still have a good life after tragedy in losing someone you love. The hope that exudes from the love that Kyle and Kendrick have deepened for Keisha, is one that we all can aspire to reach. Keisha provides useful tools to get unstuck and start on the journey of healing and finding a deeper purpose in life through loss. Keisha's ability to allow herself to be vulnerable in her story of grief and loss in order to heal the soul of another is truly transcendent. I highly recommend this book whether you have experienced loss personally or if you want to help someone you love. Either way, one cannot walk away from reading this book and not be transformed.

Alexandra Samuel-Sturgess, LCSW
Founder of Spirited By Truth

Pregnancy and infant loss is a loss like none other. No one quite prepares you for a loss of this kind. No one quite understands the arduous journey of making meaning after such a loss. This is why the text scribed by the author equates to more than just a book. It is etched by a person who knows the road of pregnancy and infant loss. Keisha writes from a place of compassion, pain, and empathy that intertwines into a riveting text that you won't want to put down. She provides a heartfelt, thoughtful, and compelling account of the varying experiences one encounters after a loss, while not categorizing everyone's experiences. Additionally, there are practical strategies provided for coping with one's feelings and creating meaning after loss.

This masterpiece is not only written for mothers. It is written for anyone who shares similar experiences or wants to support someone in loss. It is written for anyone who wants to learn about the unique experiences one goes through after a loss. It is written for you, the person who wants to feel validated, heard, seen, and transformed in your own unique way. To experience this metamorphosis in loss, please get your copy of *From Three Heartbeats to One*.

Dwayne White, LPC

As a grieving mother and the founder of the non-profit to support grieving mothers, Sunshine After the Storm, I have read a lot of books about grief. *From Three Heartbeats to One* is a unique book compared to the others that are out there. It doesn't just talk about how we are grieving and sad, it gives us useful guidance and direction on how to move beyond the pain and sadness. I think it's the best book for grieving mothers I have come across yet. Well done, Keisha. Thank you for taking your pain and creating a tool for other grieving mothers.

Alexa Bigwarfe
Author of Sunshine After the Storm:
A Survival Guide for the Grieving Mother

FROM THREE *heartbeats* TO ONE

A Gentle Companion Offering *hope* in Grieving Pregnancy and Infant Loss

KEISHA M. WELLS, LPC

Copyright © 2019 by Keisha M. Wells

From Three Heartbeats to One is published by Evan Niles Press.

All rights reserved. No portion of this book may be reproduced, stored in a retrieval system, or transmitted in any form or by any means—electronic, mechanical, photocopy, recording, scanning, or otherwise—except for brief quotations in critical reviews or articles, without prior permission in writing from the copyright owner.

While the author has made every attempt to provide accurate Internet addresses offered as citations and/or sources for further information at the time of publication, neither the author nor the publisher assumes any responsibility for errors or for changes that occur after publication.

The information provided in this book is the author's opinion and not intended to be a definitive set of instructions. Reading the information provided does not constitute a therapeutic relationship with the author and is not a substitute for mental health or medical services. This book does not address every aspect of grief and loss. Some suggestions and exercises may not apply to readers' specific needs. Please consult with a mental health or medical professional as warranted.

Scripture quotations marked KJV are from the King James Version of the Bible.

Scripture quotations marked MSG are from *The Message*. Copyright © 1993, 1994, 1995, 1996, 2000, 2001, 2002. Used by permission of NavPress Publishing Group.

Cover Design by Michelle Fairbanks
Interior Design by Lauren Lynn
Editing by Yvonne I. Kanu
Author Photography by Derrick Reed

ISBN: 978-1-7340481-0-0 (paperback)
ISBN: 978-1-7340481-1-7 (ebook)

Library of Congress Control Number: 2019952308

Printed in the United States of America
10 9 8 7 6 5 4 3 2 1

To my beloved Kyle Evan and Kendrick Niles.
My firstborn, my angels.
Because of you I've learned the core of love
and now understand the place of
loss and grief in life and living.
You've given me a great privilege—more than I could have
ever given you—to support others beyond the
stifling veil of grief.
Your sacrificial mission has been my greatest calling.
Until Eternity.

Sing, barren woman, who has never had a baby.
Fill the air with song, you who've never experienced childbirth!
You're ending up with far more children
than all those childbearing women. God says so!
Isaiah 54:1 (MSG)

Contents

Introduction	xiii
How to Use This Book	xvi
Extended Audience: Who This Book Is Also For	xvii
The Genesis of My Grief Journey	xix
The Taunting Whys, Hows, and What-Ifs	xxiii

PART I | 1

In Feeling 3
   Defining Your Emotions 4
   Being Self-Aware 10
   Identifying Dangerous Behaviors 13
   Managing Trauma and Triggers 15

PART II | 21

In Taking Care of Self: Mind, Body, and Spirit 23
   Identifying Activities for Self-Care 29
   Being Mindful: Practicing Mindfulness 32
   Forgiving Self and Others 35

PART III | 41

In Being Supported 43
   Increasing Assertive Communication 47
   Declaring Your Rights in Grieving Pregnancy
   and Infant Loss 51
   When Support Is Lacking 53

PART IV | 57

In Supporting Others: Grief and the Family   59
   Respecting Differences   63
   Communicating Effectively   65
   Parenting after Loss   67
   Helping Others   69

PART V | 73

In Defining Motherhood   75
   Still a Mother   76
   Enduring Holidays and Memorable Dates   79
   Writing a Letter to Your Beloved Baby   84
   Speaking Your Baby's Name   86

PART VI | 91

In Transforming in Loss   93
   Bearing Witness and Testifying   94
   Defining Your Story   96

PART VII | 101

In Moving Forward, Not On   103
   A Pledge of Healing in Loss   105

Affirmations at a Glance   109
Endnotes   111
Acknowledgements   113
Resources   115
About the Author   117

Introduction

I HAD YOU in mind when I started writing this piece.

The first-time mom experiencing the abrupt loss of her baby—born too soon, too small to thrive in the NICU.

The mom to an infant, a cherished being, she can no longer physically hold.

The mom facing yet another loss after enduring so many unexplained losses.

The mom whose sweet baby was born still, taking no first breaths.

The mom whose precious baby developed outside her womb.

The mom who learned early in pregnancy that her dear baby's life had ended so soon, shortly after it even began.

The mom to multiples, loving one baby in her arms and one in her heart.

The mom who has buried, in some form, all lives nurtured in her womb.

In my mind, I saw you crying in your quiet places, shielding tears at the thought of what could have been—the first steps to adore, all the birthday parties to relish, or the kisses to scraped knees. I imagined the sound of your inner thoughts—the loud, overbearing voices of failure, guilt, and shame—as you continuously blamed yourself for why your precious baby is no longer here. Your body, taunting you with the feeling and look of pregnancy but void of the life created. With your internal and external scars, I thought lovingly of you and how unbelievable this existence must be for you now—having prepared for one life to only be forced into another reality. A mother in every sense of the word to a baby you can no longer nurture, feel, or hold. A mother with so much emotion inside—so much love—yet so much misery. So empty and feeling barren.

I considered the support you deserved and would need. The care your heart would demand to survive. The space you would need to reconstruct the fragmented pieces of your broken life. I wanted you to know it is okay, vital even, to grieve and take time to cast your feelings, your questions, your doubts, into a safe space free of judgment, rhyme, or restraint. I thought of the insight and comfort you would benefit from on this soul, sole journey—one of your own individual path. I hoped knowledge and understanding could provide clarity on your path to healing and learning to live anew with the loss of your precious baby or babies. As a mom who also has buried her beloved babies, I thought compassionately of you now facing so much uncertainty ahead in this out-of-order, tragic aspect of maternity.

Introduction

The grim realities of motherhood do not match the myths we were taught to believe. As young girls playing with our favorite dolls, we looked forward to becoming mothers, to reach the pinnacle of womanhood. We grew up trusting the most esteemed honor a woman could achieve was producing life. After all, that's what a woman's body was designed to do—give birth. However, for us, when we dreamed about becoming mommies, we never envisioned the loss of a child. That the prized stuffed or plastic babies we held and cared for would not result in our own living babies to love and cherish. Believing the fantasies about motherhood, we were not warned that all babies do not live. That not all pregnancies produce thriving babies. And that not all women who desire to be a mom will create and produce life naturally and without difficulty.

The fact that approximately one in four pregnancies ends in loss was not addressed. That one woman (or one family) out of four will bear sorrow in pregnancy or infant loss[1] was not considered in those childhood fairy tales. It is not mentioned until you become familiar with your reality in a disturbing statistic. This is not the motherhood we wished for. This book was not a desired item for your baby registry. You never imagined you would need to connect with others who have experienced the loss of a baby. But here you are—here we are—with countless loss moms striving to make sense of and move forward in the greatest heartache of our lives.

HOW TO USE THIS BOOK

I created this book to be a tool of healing through insight and reflection to aid you on your grief journey. I believe it will help you because I know it would have helped me after losing my twin boys, Kyle and Kendrick, who were born prematurely in 2007. This book is a gentle, yet thought-provoking companion, from one mother in loss to another. You may be a few weeks or months on your grief journey—or perhaps years. Though our loss journeys and stories are unique, there are common emotions felt and experienced in grief and loss. Please use this resource to help, as well as motivate you to learn of additional sources of support you need and want in grieving and healing.

On the pages of this interactive book, please cast your silent cries of this altered motherhood. Give purpose to grief by reading the chapters and completing the structured exercises crafted to promote introspection, self-care, and healthy grieving. I encourage you to read, reflect, and write in an environment where you feel comfortable and secure. That space may be on your bed under the warmth of a cozy comforter; in the corner of your favorite coffee shop; beach side on a cool, clear morning; or even behind the stacks at your local library. Wherever and however, write as much or as little as needed. At the end of each chapter are prompts for reflection and affirmations for action, as well as a writing space for your thoughts and revelations. Read and work at your own pace, but do strive to complete the exercises ahead to aid you in your journey.

This book will not reference every experience you will encounter in grieving and healing in loss; however, it is written to offer support, compassion, and encouragement. Of course, only you know exactly how you feel. Only you can define the steps you will take on this path in motherhood. Grief requires your own expression and courage. Receiving support and knowledge from others who have traveled similar paths can also be beneficial. And that is why, at this time, I created this book for you.

EXTENDED AUDIENCE: WHO THIS BOOK IS ALSO FOR

My writing style may feature terms specific to women (i.e., motherhood, mama, mom) but anyone impacted by the loss of a baby who was deeply loved will benefit from reading this work. At times, I may write singularly in stating "your baby" but this book is also for a woman who has endured multiple losses such as myself. If you are a parent, grandparent, family member, or friend who seeks to gain insight to this specific loss or to comfort yourself or someone grieving a loss, you are welcome here. Professionals who work with women or families impacted by loss such as doctors, nurses, mental health clinicians, clergy, doulas, midwives, or funeral directors, desiring more knowledge to better serve your patients or clients, you are welcome here. Pregnancy and infant loss impacts us all as life is the foundation of generations. When conceptions do not occur and pregnancies and babies do not thrive—it is a global concern, one that deserves respect, empathy, and attention. We all mourn and grieve, even if in different ways and roles, which we will explore in the "In Supporting Others: Grief and the Family" section.

With effective tools and support, you can transform in grieving to heal and make meaning in loss. Please know you are not alone in this hurt. As I have learned, numerous women like me know your heart. Allow me to share a brief view of my beginnings in motherhood—the genesis of my grief journey—which led me to this moment with you. I share this glimpse into my story to provide you a sense of understanding. This connection was something I craved in my early days of grieving but was hard to find. Our losses and stories may vary but, in this hurt, we share a bond that far too many women will endure. Our truth-telling is fundamental to healing us all.

Introduction

THE GENESIS OF MY GRIEF JOURNEY

I never imagined I would be a mom to my twins, Kyle and Kendrick. That two lives would be created within mine simultaneously is such a fascinating miracle. I don't believe any woman is ever primed to realize she is a mother to twins, incubating two beings in her individual space. Even if a couple wishes for a twin conception, the moment of realization and every second going forward is a marvel to the mind. It was for me in 2006 when my unexpected twin pregnancy was confirmed. I stand in awe of it now—even as I write these words. To think, I sustained two lives inside my body. I conceived, carried, and delivered two babies. As my sons' conception was never considered, neither was their transition. My family did not have a point of reference for premature birth and loss. No one could have prepared us for the reality of burying our beloved boys.

An unlikely scenario collided into my family's plans on April 12, 2007, when I went into labor prematurely. A deep and unfixable scratch to my smooth record. I had an uneventful pregnancy, excluding my nosebleeds, extreme breast tenderness, and odd cravings for cherry slushies. Nothing alarming occurred until I learned the weird sensations and discomfort I felt in my stomach at various times that day was indeed the beginnings of labor. Prior to going to the emergency room, I called my doctor's office and explained my symptoms to the nurse. She instructed me and my family to go to the hospital just to be safe. At the hospital my contractions were not detectable on the monitor and I was about to be sent home. Once the nurse manually checked my cervix, she discovered I was dilated. At this moment, life became a blur of actions—those occurring in and outside of my body—regarding my boys' wellbeing.

Restricted, at 23 weeks gestation, I lay in a hospital bed at an adverse position with my pelvis tilted above the three of us, trembling and shaking from inside at the news that the birthing process had already began far too many weeks ahead of schedule. Far too soon. *Now? Why? How is this possible? WHAT IS HAPPENING?* Many thoughts bombarded my mind as I lay terrified but hopeful in the middle of a whirlwind of nurses, doctors, and family, all moving and talking so fast with different roles and beliefs. The on-call doctor's prognosis was grim and dire. From the outset, he explained to me and my family that survival was slim for my boys and if they did live, severe birth defects and disabilities would be likely. Of course, my family and I believed the best. One of the nurses on duty was encouraging, explaining to me how she had seen many families in our situation birth pre-term babies who survived. With faith, I believed this would be my case.

For two days, we fought in faith and on strict bedrest to halt my boys' delivery. Doctors switched my medications, took ultrasounds, and prepared for my long-term stay, while my family members visited and called, offering prayers and support. Nevertheless, my sons were delivered by an emergency C-section on April 14. As they entered the world, I was under anesthesia, unable to hear their soft, tender cries. Their lungs were so young and undeveloped—too tiny to sustain life.

Out of surgery, in another hospital room surrounded by family, I heard the worst words I have ever come to know—*They didn't make it.* In pain and shock, I sobbed briefly. My boys were not alive outside of my body. Once aware of my family members in the room, I shut my emotions off quickly and tightly like a dripping faucet. I gained my composure and switched to a woman in control of her emotions. At the time, I didn't understand the work of trauma at hand. I had separated myself from feeling, from being. Immediately, instantaneously, and without intention. This was not the report I planned to hear about my boys. I did not expect that I would not be able to see them alive, hold them alive, and take them home alive when they were healthy and strong enough to do so. There would be no bellies to tickle, no smiling cheeks to kiss. I had no idea I would leave the hospital babyless, three days after being so full of life—from three heartbeats to one. Three heartbeats once so strong and close, now only mine in a broken heart. Alone, I faced the outcome of living a life I was not prepared for without my dear boys.

Opening my eyes that Sunday morning on April 15, after the anesthesia had worn off, to realize my boys were indeed no longer present in my body or on earth, I was plowed again. I lay propped up on pillows in the hospital bed, my eyes met my deflating stomach—no longer full of life and two additional heartbeats. Tears rolled gently down my cheeks as I commented to my mom about the changes my body was quickly undergoing. My body was pregnant in some ways—and not in others—with decreasing hormones but no outer evidence or "anything to show for it." In her sadness and shock, she remained silent. So did I in mine.

This numbness extended, capturing my mind and rendering me helpless to complete simple tasks. I can recall how hard it was bathing for the first time, standing in the hospital shower naked and vulnerable before the nurse on duty. I could not bathe myself. I just stood there, physically present, but so vacant. I was in shock, allowing a stranger to do for me what I had done for myself for countless years. I didn't understand the events of those early moments as a bereaved mother. I didn't know I had detached as if someone unplugged all feeling from my body. I was in and out of my mind at the same time. Not uncommon experiences in grieving, but gravely foreign to me, and I remained that way for quite some time—through their burial, the first years without them. Family and friends often said they wanted the "old Keisha" back as they saw the major shift in my being.

I am emotionally better now, but then we didn't know I could never return as I was before. The conception, life, and transition of my boys forever changed my very core.

Perhaps you have been or are currently in the fog of trauma—moving in slow motion and standing still at the same time. Or perhaps you find yourself busy and hurried in different tasks to maintain distance from grief. You may find yourself oscillating between many states from minute to minute, which is understandable. It may not feel comfortable or normal, but it is a common occurrence in grief and loss. How can the mind and body reconcile the end of a life so desired and hoped for? The whys, hows, and what-ifs are unrelenting, taking over your thoughts. At one time, they consumed me until I sought additional support from others and began the tough work of identifying and processing my emotions, as you and I will explore in detail in Part I, "In Feeling."

THE TAUNTING WHYS, HOWS, AND WHAT-IFS

These questions are not foreign to you: *Why did this happen? How? How is this my life now?* You have asked yourself and maybe even others, time and time again, with no response or resolution. In your quiet time, with thoughts wandering, you question what happened, what didn't happen, and what could have possibly happened years from now if your sweet baby lived.

WHAT IF...
My baby was one of those who survived, defying the odds?
I went to the hospital sooner?
She stayed in my womb for a few more weeks or even days?
They were here today? They would be walking and teething now.
I could hold you outside of my womb?
I knew the sound of your cry?
You were a picky eater, hating veggies like me?
You lived to be the first college graduate of our family?
You were a parent too, providing me a world of joy in having grandbabies?

What if your heart was never shattered into so many jagged, hard-to-fit pieces? What kind of mother would you be to your baby now or years to come? Soft-hearted and easy-to-get-over-on, attending to the slightest pout or the stern, rule enforcer? You long to know. I too question who I would be if my sons were alive today. I will never know the life I desired to have with my sons. During my pregnancy, I dreamed of finally being able to kiss tender toes and smell their fresh baby scent. Enjoying sweet moments of coloring Easter eggs, hanging Christmas stockings, graduating from college, or even holding my grandbabies—their children. I longed to know. I still long to know. Forever, I can only imagine.

We did not receive the option to know how we would have raised our babies; nevertheless, our love is tangible. Our love for our babies has value. I understand your struggle in trying to make sense of the nonsensible. The unknown, coupled with your mind and heart's pull to question what might have been in your perfect world, is harrowing. The reality of burying your baby, whether that be in a physical burial or the grave of your heart, is unfathomable. It challenges your mind to question if different actions had occurred, maybe your dear baby would be here now.

Numerous moms have asked (and will continue to ask) these questions: *Why my baby? Why my family? With the numerous cases of child abuse, why did those parents receive (and neglect) the gift of life while my arms remain empty and my heart heavy? Why was my baby snatched from me?* If allowed one question to ask God, this would be my earnest inquiry: *Why does anyone have to fight and suffer to have a child?* For the women who have struggled to conceive, to the women who have fought loss after loss. From three heartbeats to one.

The fact that your child is not present, now shifts your thoughts to terrifying and aching questions: *How will I make it? How do I grieve this loss? How am I supposed to feel, to live? Function in a hurtful world with empty arms?* It's normal for you to question the many aspects of your life now. Previously, you may have been certain of your world. Now, you lack understanding as nothing makes sense at all. Acknowledging your various feelings and emotions is crucial to your grief journey. As you read these words now and have trusted me to encourage you and share my heart, I don't question the what-ifs with as much sorrow at this point on my grief journey. If not for this loss, my heart would not know and understand the brokenness you feel. And you deserve to be supported on this life path.

So, this is where our work begins in creating the *how* for your life. How to mourn and grieve to the other side of hope in living as a mom to a baby beyond your touch. You may doubt you will ever heal from this deep, unimaginable, and out-of-order pain. The short answer is yes, you will. In time, maybe sooner than you expect, your heart, so heavy now with piercing pain, will swell with love and smile at the mention of your baby. But it's important to allow the work of healthy grieving to take place. Even if on shaky ground, a step forward takes you further.

Together, we will work through feeling and understanding your emotions, as well as developing a plan to move through your pain by taking care of yourself and receiving support from others. We will also explore means for you to transform in loss by defining motherhood, telling your story of loss, and honoring your baby. This is not a path you chose for your life, but you are capable of each step it will take to move forward. I believe in your ability to make it!

PART I

Grief has many faces and the emotions experienced vary for us all. However, the common denominator in loss is that healthy grieving calls for us to be present and courageous, acknowledging our hurts on various levels—mental, physical, and spiritual.

In Feeling

THE MANY TURNS and dead ends of the deepest and most intense maze will not rival the difficult path of emotions felt in grieving the loss of a baby. It's hard to comprehend how a person can experience so many emotions simultaneously, or none at all. And with emotions occurring at random, it's easy to not want to feel and voluntarily check out from this cruel world. Still, grieving occurs whether we entreat it to do so or not. We owe ourselves and our precious ones we miss dearly to grieve. Although the tears seem to be never-ending and leave you weary, grieving is not a weakness. It will not limit you. It will not make your life worse. It will not make your pain more unbearable. It will not take from you anymore than this significant loss already has. The tears, the hurt, the agony—the wide range of feelings you experience—

come from the gift of love and connection you have with your beloved baby. During this continuous journey in healing, the emotions of grieving will likely have you feeling each pang of heartache. You may attempt to resist feeling at all, scared to lean into your emotions and acknowledge your sorrow for fear you will become stuck, never moving forward. However, the irony of grief is that failure to enter and stand boldly in your hurt and the depth of your love for your precious baby, prolongs its work and intensifies sorrow.

DEFINING YOUR EMOTIONS

When grieving, emotions can be indescribable and relentless. You may find it hard to explain or articulate the depth of your feelings. Guilt, shame, anger, and depression are common to grief and our type of loss. You may relate to these emotions and others, experiencing them as a pounding avalanche of questions, disparaging thoughts, and painful feelings. The following statements may mirror your inner dialogue. While reading you may hear your voice or feel your heart in each word:

- **Guilt**- *My body is defective. Why did it betray me? Why didn't I do this right? I should have known better. I should have done more. This is my fault. If only I had…*

- **Shame**- *I'm less than a woman. I'm not good enough to be a mom. I'm not even a real mom—I don't have a baby that others can see. My loss doesn't matter. No one understands so there's no need for me to talk about my baby.*

- **Anger**- *Why did this happen to me? To us? Why wasn't I able to have my baby? Why were my babies taken from me? Where is God for me to suffer like this? I don't deserve this! I don't believe and I don't trust anyone.*

- **Depression**- *How will I live now without my precious baby? Nothing matters. No one matters. My heart—my life—will never be the same. There is no joy without my baby.*

Grief has many faces and the emotions experienced vary for us all. However, the common denominator in loss is that healthy grieving calls for us to be present and courageous, acknowledging our hurts on various levels—mental, physical, and spiritual. I encourage you to resist the desire to block feeling the hurt, anger, disappointment, guilt, and shame in what you could not prevent. Allow yourself space to feel and receive support in facing this path in grieving. In this section, we will work to identify your emotions and feelings in creating a solid foundation for healthy grieving.

As we probe further, the following are emotions you may be familiar with on your grief journey. Take a moment to read and consider the emotions and feelings listed. Which emotions do you identify with? Place a star by the emotions you feel currently. Which emotions have been the most difficult to endure? Also, identify emotions or feelings you have experienced not listed here.

POWERLESS HOPELESS HORRIFIED CONFUSED ENRAGED SHOCKED DISGUSTED VIOLATED MISUNDERSTOOD FORGOTTEN WEARY DRAINED TRICKED TORMENTED REGRETFUL ABANDONED UNSEEN UNHEARD EMPTY PURPOSELESS NAUSEOUS NEGLECTED SORROWFUL FREAKISH UNDESERVING GUILTY BETRAYED DECEIVED UNLUCKY ASHAMED DEFECTIVE SAD FATIGUED DEAD BARREN PUNISHED TERRIFIED TRAUMATIZED DAZED NUMB DENIED CHEATED LONELY USELESS ANXIOUS BURDENED MISERABLE HEARTBROKEN HELPLESS JEALOUS BITTER ROBBED DISCOURAGED HOLLOW

Some emotions may be easier to feel such as anger or rage. Oftentimes, these emotions are covering deeper feelings and beliefs at the core such as despair, guilt, and shame. Emotions that are too grim to feel or even face are often the ones cut off.

During my first moments in loss, I turned off the faucet to my emotions to face my sudden reality as a childless mother. The emotional faucet didn't stay off for long, despite my attempt to control the despair and shock I felt at the time. You may have used the same defense mechanism. The sight of a baby or mom-to-be—the uncomfortable and jarring reminder of your loss—leaves you emotionally stumbling in pain but hiding it all behind a stone-faced veil of hurt. Trying to rationalize, you push your emotions aside: *I can't deal with this right now.* Grief does not request an opportune time for us to feel. Waiting in the checkout line at the grocery store may not be an ideal space to allow yourself the right to sob and feel the depths of your broken heart. That is correct. But, when you get to your car in the parking lot, you can let the tears flow. Or if you are in the shower and grief rises, it's okay to allow it to do so. If sitting with your closest friend and the millionth Pamper commercial comes on and you feel inclined and safe enough to do so, cry. Acknowledge your hurt and even the awkwardness of such moments. Resisting emotions will not make them go away because you do feel. And deeply. Deeper than you have ever known possible. Even in numbing, there is an undercurrent of feeling, subtle and tingling.

Use the prompts below to aid you in processing and acknowledging your emotions at this point on your grief journey. You may want to rush through or skip this section—charging ahead, lightning fast to get beyond or away from how you feel, but the feelings will never dissipate. The jagged edges in loss may dull as you grow in loss, but you will always feel. Take a moment to reflect on and complete:

- *Grieving my baby feels like _____.*

- *I numb or resist emotions when _____.*

- *I don't want others to know _____ about my feelings.*

- *It's hard for me to admit _____ about loss.*

These prompts may be hurtful to read, let alone think about. But take time with them. Sit and cry with them. Allow yourself to feel the core of your emotions. This is not the end for you. The hurt and anger you feel now in loss has the power to positively transform your life and others. You may not believe it now, but I believe you will identify with the following words on your grief journey. If you remain brave and hopeful, you will see it.

CONFIDENT LOVED JOYFUL RELAXED INSPIRED EXCITED HAPPY PEACEFUL BRAVE COURAGEOUS LOVING DETERMINED BOLD EMPOWERED WORTHY STRONG CREATIVE SAFE WELL SUPPORTED EMPATHIC TRANSFORMED RESILIENT TRANSPARENT UNDERSTOOD HEARD SEEN PROUD ENCOURAGED OPTIMISTIC VALID

Add emotions you desire to feel now and hope to experience as you move forward in loss. Losing your baby will never be a joyous fact, but the love you feel for the precious life you created will in time, if not now, bring a smile to your face. Dear loss mom, acknowledging that your baby's life has meaning and deserves to be honored will one day not feel as heavy as the forced separation of pregnancy and infant loss.

_____

_____

_____

_____

BEING SELF-AWARE

Often, when grieving, a person strives to move forward with no insight on how loss is impacting their lives and how they feel and manage such loss. Self-awareness provides a baseline in defining and understanding what and how you feel. This level of awareness and introspection is essential to navigating grief and loss. Although we may seek to end despair following the loss of our babies, it's crucial to know how we experience and manage grief and loss to move forward in a healthy manner. Take time to journal and answer the following questions. If overwhelmed with this process, it's okay to pause for a moment or come back to a question later. You do not have to answer the questions in order but strive to address each one honestly. If other questions come to mind during this exercise, please write them down and allow time for further exploration.

- *What triggers my different emotions in grieving? What sights, sounds, smells, memories, or thoughts impact me emotionally and physically?*

- *How do I respond to loss? Do I block feelings and emotions? Even when I'm alone? Do I cry when needed? Do I seek to understand how I'm feeling and why?*

- *Where do I feel grief? Body aches? Headaches? Heaviness in my chest?*

- *Is it hard for me to ask for help? If so, what stops me from seeking support?*

- *Who do I feel comfortable talking to about this loss? Who do I talk to the most about my emotions? Who has been most helpful and comforting? Who has been the least supportive and encouraging?*

- *How have I managed previous deaths, losses, and endings in the past?*

- *How do I deal with emotional pain?*

- *Am I participating in behaviors that could hinder my grief journey? Detaching and resisting emotions? Numbing emotions with drugs and alcohol, excessive spending, overeating, undereating, or dangerous sexual activity? Engaging in self-harm practices such as hair pulling or cutting my skin?*

- *What do I need others to understand and know about my grief? Speaking freely, without fear of judgment, what would I say to them?*

- *What grace do I need to extend to myself while grieving?*

IDENTIFYING DANGEROUS BEHAVIORS

There is no standard for how you should or will feel in grieving. As you know, nothing in life can prepare a mother for the depth of feeling and pain in losing a child. Grief can appear at any moment, triggered by the slightest occurrences and often with no warning. Even in not knowing what to prepare for, there are behaviors to be aware of in grieving. In the case of self-harm; harming others; thoughts, plans, or attempts of suicide or homicide; or psychosis, please seek help immediately. The following behaviors are important to note. Please seek additional treatment and intervention if you are:

- Experiencing persistent feelings of depression and hopelessness with thoughts of death and suicide.

- Experiencing persistent feelings of depression and hopelessness with a plan or attempt to harm or kill yourself or others.

- Hearing sounds, seeing visuals, feeling sensations, smelling odors, or perceiving tastes that others do not experience.

- Experiencing obsessive thoughts in which your mind

remains fixed on a topic, issue, or concern.

- Experiencing paranoid, irrational, or illogical thoughts.

- Participating in self-harming behaviors, such as hair pulling, or cutting, bruising, biting, scratching, and burning your skin.

- Engaging in risky or dangerous behaviors, including the use of alcohol, drugs (prescribed, unprescribed, or illegal), or sex that endangers your wellbeing.

You may take part in self-injurious or unsafe behaviors because of the trauma you have experienced and your need to cope with the loss. Ultimately, such behaviors will not promote grieving and healing but are used to numb and stop the pain. And in grieving, we must feel—no matter how hurtful the feelings are. Feeling is the path to mourning and grieving, which promotes healing; however, it is imperative to be safe and well in doing so.

In addition to local community mental health centers, national organizations provide support for individuals in crisis. The National Suicide Prevention Lifeline provides free and confidential emotional support, day or night, for individuals in the United States. Visit www.suicidepreventionlifeline.org for resources and contact information. The Crisis Text Line also offers confidential support for individuals in the United States and the United Kingdom via text. Visit www.crisistextline.org for more information.

MANAGING TRAUMA AND TRIGGERS

Unquestionably, losing a baby is traumatic and many moms experience shock and stress reactions following the loss. Trauma may manifest as disturbing thoughts; difficulty in falling and staying asleep; isolation; physical sensitivity or reactions to sights, sounds, and smells; and moodiness, to name several more characteristics. The fact that our pregnancies did not conclude as planned or our babies did not thrive is a traumatic experience in itself. Additionally, our babies' entries or departures in this world consisted of abrupt moments of hurt and stress. Our minds may remember all, some, or none of the details. On our grief journeys, such memories can trigger us and without notice. The faintest smell, slightest sound—a baby crying or laughing, or a song's lyrics—or image may spark intense, out-of-the-blue emotions.

Pregnancy milestones or defining dates, including dates of your baby's birth, the date of loss, or the due date may trigger or cause shifts in mood. Holidays or days and months of awareness such as October's Pregnancy and Infant Loss Awareness Month and October 15th, The Global Wave of

Light and Pregnancy and Infant Loss Remembrance Day, can also have a negative impact. The news of a loved one's pregnancy or birth announcement may be upsetting, causing you to feel sadness, anger, or possibly guilt in the lack of joy for others' celebrations. Even the sight of a hospital or thought of going to a doctor's office for a follow-up appointment post-loss can be a trigger as you imagine sitting and waiting in a sea of pregnant moms who are unaware of the torment you face in loss.

Emotional triggers can cause vast emotions from sadness and anger to panic. You may experience irritability, anxiety, fear, a strong sense of dread, and deep despair. Or you may feel nothing. At times, our minds may seem to forget the pain of loss, but our bodies recall the trauma. Emotions are unpredictable in loss. I have experienced holidays and anniversary dates where I felt such hope, love, and pride concerning my boys, but others have been debilitating. However, in learning how dates, environments, etc., impact me, I have been able to advocate for myself to make it through such moments. And you can too.

Being Grounded

Understanding your triggers is important to manage mood. Please know that triggers are manageable when identified and with adequate emotional tools. The following are self-soothing techniques you can use during anxious or tense moments. Some activities may not work for you, but you can be creative in discovering your own as this is your journey.

- For one minute, take deep and slow breaths from your abdomen. Repeat as necessary.

- Play a favorite song, soothing or upbeat.

- Chew a piece of gum or suck on a piece of hard candy such as peppermint, spearmint, or cinnamon.

- Sniff your favorite or calming essential oil to provide comfort. Oils can be carried in your purse or bag. You can also wear essential oil necklaces or bracelets.

- Enjoy a warm or soothing shower or bath.

- Exercise by going for a walk, running, or dancing.

- Focus your mind on what is taking place around you at the time of nervousness or panic. Concentrate on what you see, hear, smell, touch, and even taste. Speaking aloud (or taking notes), describe elements of your surroundings. For example, sitting in your car on a busy street, you may observe and say (or write): *I see a tall tree and a red car. I see a man carrying a brown briefcase. I hear a car engine and a car horn. I feel my shirt, a cool breeze, and the warmth from the sun on my arm. I smell perfume. I taste spearmint chewing gum.* Take slow, deep breaths, allowing yourself to be present in the moment. If necessary, speak calming, positive affirmations: *I am safe. I will be okay.*

- Journal about your feelings and triggers in the moment.

The main objective in grounding yourself is to decrease anxiety and increase calm by distracting your worried mind with the moment. Grounding techniques are beneficial when used appropriately and as needed. Overall, in feeling, be gracious and brave. Allow yourself to feel and be observant. Ask those closest to you to inform you if they notice any behaviors that are out of character, threatening, or harmful to your wellbeing.

Counseling may be helpful to manage the core issues of your grief, or prior trauma intensifying your current loss. Additionally, to decrease depressive symptoms and anxiety, antidepressants and anxiety medication may be beneficial. Please consult with a psychiatrist or your primary care physician about medication. Medications do not compensate for the powerful work of therapy and grief support. They can ease specific symptoms but will not take away grief. To find a mental health professional in your local area, you can use online directories such as GoodTherapy, Therapy for Black Girls, and Psychology Today, to name a few. If you choose to use health insurance to pay for services, you can also locate professionals via your insurance company's provider directory.

IN REFLECTING

Journal to identify, process, and keep track of what you are feeling. Journaling is a powerful tool and there are various means to do so. Hand-written or electronic app journals can be useful. Use this prompt to aid you in contemplating and writing about your emotions:

Today on my grief journey, I feel…, I believe…, I need…, I want…

_____

_____

_____

_____

IN AFFIRMING

In courage, I grieve.
I will not die in this hurt.
Grief will not defy my love.

PART II

In your hurt, you may doubt the positive impact of self-care in your life; however, self-care has its place in loss and is important to foster healthy grieving. It takes determination and intention to grieve in a healthy manner.

In Taking Care of Self: Mind, Body, and Spirit

GRIEF OFFERS NO direction to help rebuild life in the absence of your baby. Unfortunately, there is no set guide for this life, but there are practices you can start today to nurture self-care and wellness on this journey. Self-care is internal, introspective, and personal work. It's being gracious and kind to self in taking care of your mind, body, and spirit. If you recently endured a loss, I understand taking care of yourself at such a raw and intense time in grieving seems insignificant. It didn't matter to me when I came home without my boys. I questioned: *What matters now that my babies are not alive?* In your hurt, you may doubt the positive impact of self-care in your life; however, self-care has its place in loss and is important to foster healthy grieving. It takes determination and intention to grieve in a healthy manner. So, your taking care of you is necessary and serves a purpose.

Taking Care of Your Self-Talk

Be kind to yourself. Resist condemning yourself for what you are not doing, not able to do, or could not do. Resist using *shoulds: I should be, I should have, I shouldn't have.* Using should is a form of self-critique that diminishes self-esteem and self-confidence. *Shoulds* promote a feeling you are making an error in action and judgment—that you are missing the mark. *Shoulds* also cause feelings of guilt, defeat, and shame. Overall, be the best self to self you can be and eliminate toxic thinking. I know, it's beyond challenging but ask yourself: *What kind words would I have for my friend in this position, feeling the same weight of pain?* Make sure your inner dialogue manifests love and kindness for self. Work on using affirmations, positive statements, or even scriptures in how you think and speak about yourself. These are powerful tools to challenge the negative, overbearing voices that attack when one is in pain or facing conflict. As a guide, I have included affirmations at the end of each chapter. I encourage you to create your own as well. Remember this: you hear your inner dialogue all the time—more than any other voice. Work to ensure it is soothing and affirming instead of loud and critical. Be gentle with you.

Taking Care of Your Mind

When feeling overwhelmed with thoughts running wildly through your mind, try pausing for a time to be present in the moment. Remember to ground yourself by concentrating on elements of your surroundings. Using your senses, pay attention to what you see, hear, smell, touch, or taste in the moment. Meditation, mindfulness, and prayer are also helpful to quiet the mind and help you channel your thoughts. You do not have to dedicate hours to these practices, as they can be challenging concepts, but practicing for minutes at a time can benefit your overall mental health. I included mindfulness exercises later in this section to help you improve in focusing your mind.

Silence distractions to unplug and give your mind a rest. Allow yourself time away from the laptop, tablet, and cell phone notifications that constantly challenge your focus. Additionally, it's important to decrease distractions to identify and process your emotions. Such distractions can also contribute to negative shifts in mood as we become on edge, feeling compelled to follow the buzz and reply to text and email messages.

Encountering the lives of others portrayed on social media can cause emotions of anxiety, jealousy, anger, and sadness, especially when your news feeds taunt you with images of glowing moms with budding bellies and families with healthy babies. A personal time-out on social media outlets can benefit your mental health and morale. And you have the right to distance yourself from such interactions by choosing to unfollow or snooze individuals. For your peace of mind, it's okay to establish and maintain this boundary.

As I mentioned before, consider counseling support services to manage your mental health. The choice to enter a therapeutic relationship with a professional counselor or mental health clinician is a brave step, particularly in individual grief counseling, as the topics of death and loss are not easily approached. Still, counseling with a trained professional can be of great benefit to your mind and overall wellbeing. Professionals in this setting offer confidential support and education as you work to navigate your grief journey. Counselors can normalize the emotions you are feeling and work with you to manage them. For example, in this role, the counselor will help you understand and process the sudden outburst of tears you may experience when seeing diaper commercials or pregnant women. Support groups, conducted in-person or online, also foster another level of comfort and understanding as they provide an opportunity to meet with other individuals who have endured loss. The loss experiences may vary; however, the emotions often felt are universal. No matter how one participates, this sense of understanding and togetherness can promote healing and prevent isolation on the grief journey.

Taking Care of Your Body

When grieving during the postpartum period, you may experience various physical challenges such as abdominal and pelvic pain, in addition to headache, backache, and fatigue. Grief can also manifest in the body as tiredness, sleep disturbances, or chest pain attributed to stress. Bodily pains, combined with the physical aches of grief, can create an intense experience requiring physical healing. To manage grief, create a routine for wellness. Try to follow a healthy diet, eating well-balanced meals and staying hydrated by drinking plenty of water and natural juices. Meal preparation can be a helpful tool to facilitate staying on track with daily nutrition. In addition to eating and drinking well, strive to maintain adequate sleep and physical rest, as both promotes a healthy immune system and improved mood. If possible, establishing a routine for sleep such as taking a soothing shower, meditating, using aromatherapy, or dimming the lights in the bedroom at a specific time each night, can create a more welcoming sleep environment.

Movement is also necessary. No matter the method of movement or exercise, such as walking, aerobics, weight training, and yoga, the key is to be active to increase positive chemicals in the brain and foster a routine of self-care. Acupuncture or body massage may also be beneficial. Overall, when the body is routinely active, stress decreases and positive mood increases. It's essential to perform routine physical exercise if able. The more you resist, the more it's needed. These areas fail as priorities when grieving; however, with a few small steps daily, you can work to achieve physical wellness.

Taking Care of Your Spirit

Loss permeates to the core and will impact every part of your being, including spiritually. Nurturing your spirit is deep work and may include practicing forgiveness; working through trying emotions and core beliefs in loss; and connecting with a higher power or elements of nature via prayer or meditation. Forgiveness is a higher call and we will explore it later in this section as it is a heavy topic that requires consideration. Gratitude, or appreciating what remains, is another important facet in cultivating your spiritual core as it challenges you to be thankful in the present moment. Practicing gratitude daily may seem inconceivable and cause you to ask yourself: *What do I have to be grateful for when my baby is not alive, in my arms?* When faced with this harsh reality, gratitude may be fleeting, especially if you are striving to manage your emotions. It is a demanding task but possible. A few things to think about and appreciate—even during this major life transition: *Do I have the support of a friend or family member? Have I received a genuine and kind word, card, text, or prayer? Am I able to read these words now to see the letters on the page?* Even the brief time you shared with your baby is a moment you will come to treasure and be grateful for in the absence of memories not to come.

IDENTIFYING ACTIVITIES FOR SELF-CARE

The list below features activities to help you in conceptualizing what self-care can look like for you. For many individuals, particularly women, being *self-full* is a foreign concept, as society often teaches girls to comply and think of others before thinking of self. However, in the courageous act of grieving, caring for and relating to self is a critical need as you heal from the inside out. Self-care starts with you. Review these activities, placing a star by any that interests you. Also, take a few moments to create your own activities. If this task is overwhelming, think back to the most carefree chapter of your life and the activities you enjoyed at that time. Hopefully, this reflection will provide insight.

- Say NO! Stop being everything to everyone but you! Focus on what you need and want by saying no to doing tasks for (or fulfilling the needs of) others.

- FEEL. Cry when needed and laugh as warranted. Resist stifling or detaching from your emotions. Allowing yourself to grieve is a form of self-care.

- Enjoy a leisurely walk in the neighborhood or at a park.

- Drink a warm, flavored tea or coffee. Rely on your favorite blend or try a new, exotic flavor.

- Take an uninterrupted bath, complete with bath oils, aromatic candles, and your favorite soap or body wash.

- Listen to your favorite album or playlist of songs. If you do not have a playlist that lifts your mood, now is a great time to create one.

- Read a magazine from cover to cover. Enjoy a classic work of literature or your favorite comic strip.

- Take a nap during the day. Yes! Even without completing all your must-do tasks.

- Enjoy a professional body massage focusing on your aching or trouble spots.

- Reconnect with a favored pastime. Remember how much you enjoyed scrapbooking as a teen or assembling a 1000-piece puzzle?

- Try a new recipe. Even if cooking is not your thing, creating and trying new foods can be an enjoyable experience or experiment.

- Enjoy a meal with a friend. Connect with those you can be yourself with—those who will not shy away from you and your emotions.

- Create. Tap into your artistic side and paint, draw, color, write, sew, dance, sing, or build. Find an artistic outlet to express yourself.

- Go for a bike ride, manual or motor.

- Enjoy a picnic, indoor or outdoor.

- Take a hike. Literally. Visit a state park and enjoy nature on an incline.

- Visit a botanical garden. Engage your senses taking in the vegetation.

- Enjoy a swim in your private pool, at the local gym, or beach side.

- Indulge in a sweet treat or the most decadent dessert you can find.

- Start a new television series or binge watch a season of your favorite show.

BEING MINDFUL: PRACTICING MINDFULNESS

Mindfulness, being of present mind and in the moment, is a form of meditation. Meditation has positive emotional and physical benefits including de-stressing and decreasing anxiety but can be a tricky practice to grasp at first. A multitude of thoughts often flood our minds throughout the day and for some of us, even during times of rest or sleep, it is hard to still our minds and refocus them. Often, we are multitasking, handling many things at once, or thinking about the future or past. Rarely do we find ourselves present *in* the actual moment—*in* the comfort and security of the moment.

This section features two mindfulness exercises you can try to help develop this practice if you have not mastered meditation. Be patient in adapting this skill if you are new to this form of mental direction. As with any behavior, such as being consistent in an exercise regimen, practice increases the skill. Also, please consider and ensure your physical and emotional safety when practicing any form of mindfulness or meditation.

Minding Your Senses

Choose an activity that you do daily such as showering, eating, or even doing chores. During this activity, focus on using your senses in the moment. Let's explore what being mindful in the shower could look like as a daily practice.

As you enter the bathroom and prepare for your shower, take a deep breath to relax and focus on what you see, hear, smell, touch, and even taste in these moments. Try to use all senses, if possible. For example, feel the porcelain bathtub or tile shower, the shower handle as you turn on the water. Listen to the sounds of the shower as you hear the running water. Notice how the water beads on the shower curtain or glass door. See and feel the water as it touches and trickles down your skin. Pay attention to the water's temperature and pressure, while feeling the soapsuds and lather on your skin. Feel the washcloth or sponge's texture as you rub it on your body. Breathe in the scents of soap and shampoo. You may even taste the water in your mouth as it cascades over your face.

The main idea for this practice is to concentrate on what you are doing in the moment to decrease stress and the tendency to entertain thinking about the past or an unsure future. You can also use this practice for more individual activities such as combing your hair or putting on lotion.

Mindful Visualization

Please read and become familiar with the following exercise. You will need to be in a safe, comfortable, and quiet space, using your focus and imagination. It may help to close your eyes or focus on an image as you envision yourself at the beach. You can also use a sound machine featuring sounds of rain, the ocean, or white noise. Be sure to pay attention to each breath as you inhale and exhale. This exercise is not a strict guide, but it gives you a starting point in practicing mindfulness. In building this skill, you can choose to visualize yourself in any tranquil setting.

> Imagine you are enjoying a sunny day lounging on the beach listening to the calming sounds of the ocean. Sitting on your favorite beach towel and engaging the environment with your senses, note the surrounding scene from the birds on land and in the air, to the smell of the ocean, to seashells resting at the water's edge. Observe the peaceful and gentle turquoise and emerald waves before you. Take a moment and notice the water as it gently rolls to the shore. See the clear, blue sky and pillow-like clouds overhead. Feel the breeze and warm sun hitting your shoulders and back. Feel the soft, cool white sand and allow yourself to be in the moment, relaxed by the lulling water.

Overall, commit to making time each day to have quiet moments to focus your mind. Remember this: mindfulness may be difficult at first, so start small and be patient. To decrease stress, try practicing mindfulness one minute at a time during both moments of calm and worry.

FORGIVING SELF AND OTHERS

Forgiveness is for YOU—not the person who needs to be forgiven.

You have probably heard this statement (or similar) and cringed, thinking to yourself: *How do I forgive the most profound hurt in my life? How do I forgive others for their hurtful words, or their silence? How do I forgive the medical professionals for callous statements made? For reducing my most precious gift to a medical casualty? For diminishing my concerns, denying my maternal instinct? How do I forgive those who minimized my loss because it occurred in the first trimester? How do I forgive myself for the blame and guilt I feel? Why should I forgive those who have never asked for forgiveness?*

There are many deep hurts to forgive in pregnancy and infant loss, and it takes time and effort to heal such wounds. The weight of unforgiveness is a heavy burden that can disrupt your spirit and work against you unknowingly as you strive to grieve and heal. Unforgiveness breeds resentment, rage, and pain, which can block your growth journey through loss. Let's bravely take a closer look at the daily practice of forgiving self and others.

I forgive is an affirmation—an act of faith. When we say we forgive someone or ourselves, it is a statement made even if the feeling is lacking. Even if the offense is too great to comprehend or pardon. We say it and believe it as a declaration that although I do not like the outcome, I choose to forgive what I could not change or stop. I choose to forgive what you did (or did not do). Forgiveness does not invalidate your hurt or feelings. Forgiveness does not excuse the issue. Forgiveness means you accept the outcome was not wanted, anticipated, planned for, believed, asked for, or even deserved. This is a massive order to process, especially when one is treated unfairly, left with unresolved feelings, and lacks an understanding of what happened in loss. Please understand, I know these words are simply read and may be hard to process now. Why should you forgive what is unjust? What is not right? Not warranted?

It is difficult to forgive others, granting them mercy despite their unkind comments or actions. But often, the greatest—and most difficult—one to forgive is self. Forgive yourself for what you did not know or did not do. Forgive yourself for what you did know and did do. Forgive yourself for every lie you believed about yourself. Forgive yourself for beating up you—instead of loving and nurturing you. Forgive yourself for believing the losses you have endured signify your abilities and worth. The more you condemn yourself, the deeper unforgiveness will burrow inside of you. Be gentle with your heart and view of self. Be bold in extending grace to yourself.

To process and release the emotions you feel, the unforgiveness you have towards self and others, consider writing a letter to the person who has offended you—even yourself. Express every detail of your feelings from hurt to rage. Write unfiltered with no form, to allow yourself full expression. You may articulate all you feel in one sitting or it may take several encounters to fully express and release your emotions on the page. Forget grammar, spelling, and punctuation. When you have completed the task or a draft, read it aloud. Allow yourself to feel. Hold nothing in or back. Complete this task for those who hurt you such as friends, family members, doctors, nurses, and coworkers. After you read the letter, you may choose to tear it into small pieces, throw it away, burn it, or revise it and give it to the person to whom the letter was written. The following are prompts to help you:

- *I'm offended by _____.*

- *I'm hurt because you did or did not _____.*

- *It upset me when you _____.*

- *I forgive you for _____.*

- *I forgive myself for _____.*

Be patient with yourself and know that forgiveness is a heavy, daily act and may take time. However, it is costlier to not forgive. With effort and grace, I hope you surrender the hurt in your heart to transform in loss.

IN REFLECTING

You can take care of and advocate for you. Create a plan to nurture and make your mental, physical, and spiritual wellbeing a priority. Ask yourself: *What activities do I need to increase or decrease daily, weekly, and monthly? What is my vow to take care of myself in grieving?*

_____

_____

_____

IN AFFIRMING

I will care for myself by _____.
Today, I will practice being still.
Today, I am grateful for _____.
Today, I choose to forgive _____.

PART III

Draw strength in knowing that, although you did not desire this outcome of loss, you can grieve in your own fashion. Even as unpredictable as grief is, you have the right to dictate what is best for you day-by-day and minute-by-minute, and you can speak to others about that.

In Being Supported

She's in a better place now.
God needed another angel.
Time heals all wounds.
You can try again.
It wasn't meant to be.
God knows best.
I know how you feel. I was so depressed when....

IT IS LIKELY that someone—a well-intended loved one, a medical professional, or even an acquaintance—spoke similar words or clichés to you as an attempt to provide comfort. How can your baby not being in your arms be a better place? How can a parent and child physically separated, even before life could thrive, be a greater outcome? Grief and loss are natural elements of life but we often handle such subjects inappropriately. We don't speak well on loss. And the strain of grief is even more severe and scathing when the loss is unexpected such as the death of a baby. It is commonly said but accurate: as parents, we never planned to bury our children. So how do we handle such challenges in communicating our sorrow to others and, most importantly, in being supported and understood by those who have no point of reference for the depth of our grief?

In trying to offer encouragement, people may say—unknowingly—inappropriate statements. Comments or condolences can sting though not said to hurt you. The mothers, fathers, spouses, partners, grandparents, siblings, aunts, uncles, and cousins to angel babies, is a select tribe. Only our members can fully comprehend our hurt. Though we may lack words to describe the chasm of loss, we know the feelings. We understand our loss. We know that just because people mean well, their words or actions are not always soothing because they lack the context for our hurt. In identifying what you need from others and how they can provide comfort at this point on your grief journey, reflect on the following questions and prompts.

- *How would I describe my grief to someone unaware of pregnancy and infant loss?*

In Being Supported

- *Who encourages me the most? What actions or gestures have they made that have been meaningful?*

- *What do I need from others during this time?*

- *How have I been disappointed in grieving? Who has disappointed me?*

- *I want _____ to know _____ about how I feel and what I need now.*

- *It comforted me when _____.*

- *What boundaries do I need to establish and maintain in my relationships?*

Please use these questions and prompts to evaluate the quality of your support system. Is your support system working or lacking guidance? If working, how so? If not, what do you need and from whom? Why? What needs to take place for change to occur?

_____

_____

On my grief journey, I have learned—albeit the hard way—that I have the right to grieve how I choose, in the healthiest way for me at the time. Often, that right includes me educating others about my needs and preferences. Initially, I resented being in this role, assuming others would intuitively know the best way to encourage me. *I'm the one bearing the full weight of my loss, can you not support me? Can you not understand what I need without me having to say so?* The short answer is no. Even in striving to be well and take meaningful steps on the path of grief, we too bear the responsibility of communicating to others what we need or do not need—what is and is not working. We also have the right to say we don't know exactly what we need, but we would like care of some sort. Grieving the loss of a child offers no model for this product of life, but we do have the right to dictate our needs and wants assertively.

INCREASING ASSERTIVE COMMUNICATION

Grieving requires assertive behavior, allowing you to speak up and advocate for yourself in owning and expressing your rights, feelings, and needs. For many individuals, speaking assertively is intimidating as it is a direct but respectful form of communication. Particularly for women, assertiveness can be difficult as we are often taught to accommodate others, denouncing or minimizing our voices: *Be seen and not heard… That's not ladylike.* In conflict, we may keep quiet because we "don't like confrontation" or we expect others to know our needs and wants. In grief work, assertiveness is key. Maintaining a passive, non-confrontational or aggressive and overbearing voice, can be detrimental to self and our relationships. Let's review examples of passive, assertive, and aggressive behaviors.

- **Passive Voice**- *My views, wants, needs, feelings, and opinions don't matter compared to those of others. I don't have the right to use my voice.* This form of communication, or the lack of, can lead to unresolved interpersonal issues and diminished self-esteem. Stifling your voice for the comfort of others can eventually erupt into aggressive communication.

- **Aggressive Voice**- *My views, wants, needs, feelings, and opinions matter more than those of others. I have the right to use my voice—others don't. Only my voice matters.* This form of communication is oppressive and can annihilate others, ultimately pushing them away. Aggressive communication can occur when a person is thinking linear, only taking their perspective into consideration, or having difficulty in expressing the core of their emotions.

Passiveness and aggressiveness are on opposite ends of the communication spectrum, lacking true resolve and respect for all parties involved.

- **Assertive Voice**- *My views, wants, needs, feelings, and opinions matter, and those of others do too. I have the right to use my voice.* Assertiveness is in the middle of the spectrum where every voice, including the voice of self, matters. At the core of assertiveness is respect. Even with differing opinions, assertive communication is optimal as it recognizes the rights and views of self and others. With this mindset, each person has the right to believe as they choose.

What is your communication style? Are you passive, aggressive, assertive, or passive-aggressive? Why? Who taught you how to communicate? On this grief journey, being assertive is helpful as you allow yourself to feel, believe, and communicate without diminishing your voice. Assertive communication is clear and empowering. Identify areas where increasing assertive communication can benefit you. Maybe you are frustrated with and need to speak to the coworker who asks personal questions or offers the question of pity: *How are you really doing?* Maybe you notice a divide in your relationship with your spouse and want them to be physically and emotionally present. Even without saying much when you are together, you desire to decrease the level of distance. If so, please know you have the right to make a request.

Draw strength in knowing that, although you did not desire this outcome of loss, you can grieve in your own fashion. Even as unpredictable as grief is, you have the right to dictate what is best for you day-by-day and minute-by-minute, and you can speak to others about that. Being assertive may call for tough conversations or even confrontations, but you can master this communication. Speaking from a place of confidence and ability, versus anger, weakness, and control, is paramount for assertiveness. And the people with whom you are communicating may be grateful for the gentle nudge on whether their actions are helpful (or not). Others may genuinely want to help but lack insight on how to best care for you. Adversely, some people lack empathy and manners—or "home training"—and need to be challenged in their rudeness. We can be a direct and helpful voice educating others to bring more awareness to what parents and families need in pregnancy and infant loss.

To assist you in fostering a positive and open voice during conversations about your needs, dislikes, or preferences in being supported, below are helpful ways to speak assertively:

- *I know you didn't intend to offend me. I felt hurt because _____.*

- *It is helpful when you _____.*

- *I feel supported when you _____.*

- *I value your support. I want you to know that I need _____.*

- *I want you to know that I prefer _____.*

- *Thank you for your help but, during this time, I want you to _____.*

- *I understand and respect your intentions to help; however, I prefer you help me by/or in this way _____.*

- *The best way you can help me now is to _____.*

- *Thank you for being patient with me. Even if I don't know how to tell you what I need or want, it helps me to know you are available.*

This concept of self-advocacy may be a lot to take in at once. Think about how you want and need those closest to you to show up in your life. When interacting with others, please know you have rights in grieving, and they matter. With this mindset, you can cultivate the support you value.

DECLARING YOUR RIGHTS IN GRIEVING PREGNANCY AND INFANT LOSS

Use the following statements to affirm your rights in grieving. Take time to read and recite them regularly, as well as create rights of your own. You can also share them with family members and friends to provide education and understanding about your grief journey.

- *I have the right to be devastated and heartbroken in grief.*

- *I have the right to grieve the loss of my baby for the rest of my lifetime. My grief and my love do not have a limit.*

- *I have the right to qualify my grief. Other people do not have the right to dictate how I should (or should not) feel or grieve.*

- *I have the right to feel a mix of emotions—those I understand and can identify, as well as those that I cannot—without providing an explanation.*

- *I have the right to prioritize my self-care and preserve my mental, emotional, spiritual, and physical energy.*

- *I have the right to say no to conversations, events, or experiences that may be hurtful or cause me emotional discomfort.*

- *I have the right to grieve my baby how I choose and when I choose.*

- *I have the right to grieve my baby without filtering my raw emotions to make other people comfortable.*

- *I have the right to name my baby and speak my baby's name.*

- *I have the right to acknowledge and honor my baby's lifetime.*

WHEN SUPPORT IS LACKING

Not every mom or person impacted by pregnancy and infant loss is supported by family and friends. Loss mom, if you are in an unstable relationship or a single mother who does not have a relationship with the person you planned to parent with, please know you still deserve support. The loss of your baby is "not for the best" because you are single. Your aching hurt is valid and there are shoulders that will bear the weight of your loss. Please consider, as discussed before, using the different support services such as counseling groups either in-person or online, or individual counseling. Clinicians offer counseling in various formats to provide more accessibility to clients. Please review the resources provided in this book as I selected them with you in mind. You don't have to suffer in isolation. Support groups vary and need to be a good fit, but they are a viable option in receiving the support you need if you are open to it. For a newcomer, it requires bravery and even transparency to take part, but positive group outlets will respect your right to share or not. Sometimes just being around others who have experienced similar pain can decrease isolation and a belief that no one understands. There is a powerful synergy when those enduring similar losses come together to support one another. I hope you will be open to using such outlets if you are not currently connected because your loss matters.

IN REFLECTING

Ask yourself: *Who supports me? How do I want to receive support? How do I receive love? Do I need to hear words of support or encouragement? Do I need help with tasks? Someone to help me do chores or errands? Do I need a hug or someone to hold me and let me cry? Do I need company? Someone to be near, even if silent? Someone to listen to me?*

_____

_____

_____

_____

IN AFFIRMING

I have the right to use my voice in loss.
I will honor my grief journey by _____.
My grief journey is unique.

PART IV

Just as you have no rhyme or reason for your hurt, just as you may have difficulty in feeling, the same could be said for your loved ones. Your presentation of grief and mourning may not resemble that of others, but that does not mean they do not feel the depth and severity of the loss.

In Supporting Others: Grief and the Family

How do I support you in this hurt when I don't know how I will make it? When I can't make it better for you or for me? When I can't change the outcome for our family? How will we rebuild our lives to create and hope again in the face of a demolished future? How can we live boldly and hopeful that we will never see this loss again when we didn't ever plan to see it?

THE PATH IN grieving is undefined and made even more complex in attending to and living with your loved ones' hurt. Sometimes, we become so focused on (and worried about) how others are managing grief, we forget about self.

Grieving your cherished baby is a walk you must endure, taking each step at a time, but you do not grieve in isolation. As you know, losing your baby impacts the family unit. Fathers, spouses, partners, grandparents, siblings, aunts, uncles, cousins, and even friends feel the various crushing emotions of loss. Still, each family member may experience the loss in unique ways. Just as you have no rhyme or reason for your hurt, just as you may have difficulty in feeling, the same could be said for your loved ones.

Your presentation of grief and mourning may not resemble that of others, but that does not mean they do not feel the depth and severity of the loss. To date, I have never seen my grandmother, Esther, cry about my sons. I have seen tears form in her eyes and heard her voice tremble at the mention of their names. But I know she has cried, and the loss is profound for her. Because of our special bond, her heart feels a deep sorrow—one I do not comprehend as I am not yet a grandmother—in the fact that we did not have the pleasure of raising our sweet Kyle and Kendrick. Rather than tears, I see her display love by supporting all things concerning her angel great-grandsons. From attending the annual March for Babies walk, fundraising for the family's March for Babies team, to going with me to the cemetery to decorate their marker—so many tangible ways she has helped me face mourning while shouldering her hurt through the years. It's an unspoken hurt, but it's there. She grieves in her way and I accept that.

My mom, Edith, who worked to physically, emotionally, and spiritually take care of me during my loss and plan the funeral for her firstborn grandchildren, initially had no time to mourn her loss. She stood outside of my hurt so doubly wounded and burdened in not being able to fix her child's hurt and her's as well. She offers the following words on her perspective in loss. Perhaps it will give you context and understanding as your family grieves now, both individually and collectively.

> As a mother, the hardest thing I have ever had to do was watch my daughter grieve the loss of her twin sons. My grief was compounded as I was also grieving the loss of my precious grandsons. What can you say to your child to heal the hurt? Witnessing her pain was heart-wrenching. To hear her say she was going home without her babies—with nothing to show for her caesarian scar was unbearable. However, I had to push my grief aside and be strong for her. The days and weeks following were tough as I put my pain away to make sure she had what she needed. When I was alone, I cried, and I was angry, but I was determined to accept what God had allowed. I still held onto my faith in God and stood on my favorite scripture, Romans 8:28: "And we know that all things work together for good to them that love God, to them who are the called

according to his purpose" (KJV). I did a lot of praying. I remember the many difficult decisions I had to make on her behalf. The many hard phone calls and conversations that had to take place: calling my boss; her boss; the hospital and doctor billing departments; the funeral home and cemetery; and relatives and friends. My maternal instinct was activated just like a bear protecting her cub from well-meaning people and their comments: *She is still young. She can have another baby. God has a lesson in every trial.* While this is true, no other child she will give birth to will ever replace our precious angels. As their grandmother, I had dreams and plans too. I dreamed of taking my boys to church and teaching them to know God. The many places we would go and memories we would create at the park, taking vacations, shopping, and going to school for the first time. I even envisioned them getting old enough to spend time with me in my yard, cutting grass. I pictured them growing up to be awesome men of God. But even during my pain and grief now, God has been true to His word and Romans 8:28 has come to pass. Our loss has blessed and helped many through our families' work with March for Babies and my daughter's counseling practice. Also, when I hear of someone losing a baby, my heart goes out to them. I pray for them and, if possible, I send a card just to let them know they are not alone. I believe God can and He will heal our hurt. Our angels will not be forgotten.

RESPECTING DIFFERENCES

Do you doubt your loved ones are grieving because you have not seen them cry or express direct sadness because of the loss? Or maybe you don't believe your family members and friends are handling loss appropriately because their response to grief varies from yours. It's not uncommon to wonder about how your loved ones are managing loss. There is no criterion for grieving. We cannot predict how we will react to or be impacted by loss, so how can we expect others to know how they will grieve? How can we critique another person's grief journey?

Though you may not understand why or how your loved ones grieve in a particular manner, work to respect the differences in how you all are adapting to living with this loss. Be open to the possibility that grief work is still taking place even if you cannot see it. Beyond your view, your loved ones may shed powerful tears or express deep rage in solitude; yet, your grief may be more transparent and in the open. Dismiss gender stereotypes, understanding that each person feels and displays grief differently. Assuming or expecting your loved ones to act in specific ways you deem suitable for grieving may stunt your healing as well as theirs. Few words may be spoken, but grief reactions may show up as extended hours in the gym; taking on extra projects at work or church; doing new and uncommon activities and hobbies; and spending more time alone in activities such as scrolling social media and surfing the Internet.

When grieving our babies, we may seek a place to put our hurt—a container to transfer the energy of our pain and grief. It may manifest as being fixated on or preoccupied in an activity, but it's an attempt to keep busy, to move forward from the hurt we feel in not having our babies. This containment may seem odd, beyond the norm, and not make sense to others or even to you, but it's an effort to make sense of the illogical. It's like maintaining your footing in a long, dark, and narrow hallway. You are constantly striving to move towards the exit of your grief, to make it to the end of the dark feelings of loss. While trying to gain your footing in grieving, you may stumble and be unsure of what you feel, grasping at everything and nothing. At times, because you fear moving forward, you may come to a standstill, unable to take another step as you are uncertain of the next shift or move of grief. This may be the same experience for your loved ones. With empathy, be patient and understand that grieving is an individual and unscripted process. You cannot predict it for yourself or others.

COMMUNICATING EFFECTIVELY

Clarity and sincere communication are central to any healthy relationship. Hopefully, your relationships have a solid foundation to communicate openly and deeply about grief and loss. No other time than when you are hurting and scared, feeling so many raw emotions, is it important for you to draw closer to others rather than retreat from them. And this can be so trying for parents, especially if emotions of blame and guilt set in and plot to take over. The feelings of failure and letting others down are like a dull ache—always present and nagging. When such thoughts lead to negative feelings and behaviors, it's important to challenge your beliefs and not allow them to take over as they can shift your mood, relationships and, ultimately, your definition of self. It's important for you to not bury negative thoughts, but acknowledge and challenge them with reality. Had you been able to change this outcome, you would have. We all would have, sacrificing anything—everything—for our babies to live. So many feelings and beliefs remain unsaid or assumed in grieving if one is not intentional in creating meaningful dialogue with others. For instance, broaching talks on how to discuss loss with your older children, to deciding when or if you will try to conceive again, requires vulnerability and compassion, so be patient with yourself and your loved ones on their grief journeys. To bond with and understand them, consider using the following prompts, questions, and statements to help spark dialogue or needed conversations:

- *I feel _____.*

- *I want _____.*

- *I need _____.*

- *I like it when you/we _____.*

- *I feel _____ when/because _____.*

- *I will support you by _____.*

- *What do you need from me?*

- *I love and care for you.*

- *I will not leave you.*

- *I'm here with you. I'm here for you.*

The questions featured in "Being Self-Aware" may also be helpful in fostering understanding and meaningful conversations with your loved ones. Consider sharing the questions and allowing your loved ones time to complete them individually and at their own pace. Overall, being certain that you are loved, supported, and cared for is essential. Understand silence speaks volumes as well. Simply being present for one another can be a balm when you cannot articulate the core of your hurt, when there are no new words to say. With time, grace, and insight, you (and those you desire to support and receive support from) can develop the language to articulate your grief.

PARENTING AFTER LOSS

Children and adolescents experience a mix of feelings such as excitement, joy, and even sadness or anger, with the news of an addition to the family. When loss arrests the family's plans, along with a child's thoughts about becoming a sibling, emotions and grief reactions can vary. Depending on the age of your older child(ren), the loss of their sibling may impact them differently. Younger children may ask questions, confused about what the loss of their sibling means for them and the family overall. Children who are older in age and knowledgeable on death and pregnancy may be quiet, lacking the words to say and avoiding the change in the family structure. Nevertheless, children feel, grieve, and notice their parents' moods and emotional shifts.

As we experience countless losses throughout our lifetimes and feel guilt and shame as a result of such deficits, it may be beneficial to explain to your child that this loss was not their fault. Using language appropriate for your child's age is helpful when explaining that pregnancy and infant loss is a horrible occurrence that affects numerous families and often without cause. Be patient with your child's grief responses (or lack of) and means to manage grief. Share with your child that crying and feeling sadness or anger are normal in the grieving process. Be sure to nurture and make your child feel loved and safe. Consider individual and group counseling or therapeutic grief camps to assist your child in processing and making meaning in loss. Additionally, creating family traditions in which your child honors their angel sibling are also effective in healthy grieving.

Self-care is imperative in parenting. Give yourself permission to feel a mix of emotions while grieving and parenting. It is normal to feel great love and pride for your living child(ren), along with deep sorrow for your angel baby. Longing for your baby and what was to be does not make you ungrateful for your present family. Your baby is a treasured member of your family and you will always remember this and desire that physical connection. As angel moms, we often feel joy and pain. Recognizing this fact prevents false guilt and shame.

HELPING OTHERS

Your loss, your hurt, and your voice matter in supporting others. At this time, you may not believe in the impact your voice can make in helping yourself and others heal, in addition to reducing stigma in pregnancy and infant loss. Grieving the loss of our children defies us to love in the face of loss; to honor and celebrate the lives we created; and to believe that our loss is not in vain. However, there is power in bonding with others who have been hurt in the way we have been hurt.

Purpose can develop in pain, and you can be a source of hope for others. Perhaps, someone else needs to see your face, needs to see your tears, needs to see you moving forward and not being stifled by the greatest hurt one can ever know. Envision how you can be a source of encouragement or hope for another person, in and outside of your family, dealing with loss. Your service to others does not have to expand continents and reach thousands of lives. If you say a kind word to another grieving parent, please know that compassionate gesture may be needed to foster healing. It is aspirational to think of your loss in this manner—that you will wear a badge of honor, metaphorically, and willfully assume the role of supporting others. It was not a chosen task, but it is doable, and for many parents, it adds depth to their loss. You did not choose grief and loss, but you do have all the power to use it for a higher purpose.

IN REFLECTING

Ask yourself: *Am I respecting my loved ones' grief journeys? Am I communicating effectively? How can I improve? Am I attending to my child's needs in loss? How can I serve others?*

_____

_____

_____

_____

IN AFFIRMING

My grief journey is not in vain.
I respect grieving is an individual path.
I will smile again.

PART V

No person can define this form of motherhood for you. No one has the right to tell you that your motherhood is invalid because your precious baby is no longer in your womb or arms. It is your distinction to acknowledge.

In Defining Motherhood

MOTHERHOOD IS COMPLEX for us. More so than we ever imagined it would be. It is not clear-cut or easily defined. It is sometimes more sorrowful than sweet but also real, valid, and enduring. As we prepare to explore how you will define motherhood and honor the life of your baby, give some thought to the following questions: *How will I mother my precious baby who is now beyond my grasp? What does motherhood mean for me? What can this life look like for me and my family after enduring the unimaginable? How will I handle the birthdays, holidays, and other dates associated with my baby? How will I love my baby from afar with all that I am and allow others to do so? How will I manage the difficult questions or situations involving others who do not understand my hurt?*

The answers to such questions are clothed in an infinite amount of patience, grace, self-love, and self-compassion. Be loving to yourself, knowing this was not the storyline you planned for or dreamed of, but you can define how you grieve and build a life acknowledging the life you created. Mama, mother, mommy, or mom applies to you.

STILL A MOTHER

Weeks following my caesarean, I was at home by myself, sitting in front of the computer and making a picture collage of my boys, using a scripture and the few precious moments captured with them. In that space, I decided to take deliberate action to not let them fade away in our daily lives. I can see that moment so vividly in my mind and feel my conviction and commitment that our family would always remember and celebrate their lifetimes—no matter how brief. And that is so powerful for an angel mom to realize. Our babies do not have to disappear into the backgrounds of our lives. They do not have to be a taboo topic or shameful part of life that did not go right. Their lifetimes are precious and valued.

That day, I decided we would give that fact meaning. We would always acknowledge our roles to our angels. At that moment, I had not considered how moms like me navigate the tricky conversations of motherhood, such as dealing with an acquaintance making small talk and asking casual but truly personal questions that blindside you: *So, how many children do you have? Do you have kids? No kids? You don't want kids? What are you waiting on? You're not getting any younger!* No matter if you are days or months on your grief journey, you too will encounter—more than once—staggering and mood-shifting questions that will challenge and probe into your motherhood.

As a new angel mom, I battled with how to answer, even though I knew I had the right to do so. Despite being self-conscious, I had to learn how to manage the unpredictability of such inquiries. How to not denounce my title of mother because I have not yet carried and birthed a child to full term. I was forced to consider: *How do I respond in a way that doesn't shatter me but is accurate, not denying myself or my boys? How do I educate this person on the reality and prevalence of pregnancy loss and infant death?* I had to determine how to navigate this channel in loss and have had many experiences thus far. I recall in graduate school, raising my hand when the professor asked the parents in class to do so in relation to his lecture topic. Feeling somewhat strange at that moment, I raised my hand in the air—*Yes, I am a mother*—instead of lowering my head. Since awkward had to be in the room, I allowed it but only with the truth—not shame.

Since that day, I have grown in motherhood. However, I must admit, depending on who asks and what mood or frame of mind I am in for the day, such inquiries still have the potential to vex me and occasionally I am taken aback. The harmless intention behind their questions still translate as a violation and intrusion, a blissful ignorance for some that the path to motherhood and parenting is complicated—defined by more than a simple, yes or no answer. And then there are instances when I am pleased to educate others and will share my story or even speak about my sons in the present tense: *Yes, I'm a mother of twin boys.* Though their queries serve as a stark reminder that my angels' role in my life and family lacks a tangible presence for others to see and make sense of, I am still a mother. My caesarian scar proves this fact. Each tear shed—silent or visible—is proof enough. And most important is the smile in the beat of my heart when I reflect on the gift of their lives.

Even when faced with well-intended but ultimately gut-wrenching questions, I am still Kyle and Kendrick's mom. That is my declaration. What do you declare? I acknowledge motherhood daily—not just on Mother's Day or my sons' birthday. I am a mom and will forever be because they made me so. Their lives forever changed my status. It is settled. I do not suggest the path I'm traveling in motherhood as the one you should take. I simply offer my awareness as an option for you because so many moms believe they must denounce their identity and experience in motherhood. No person can define this form of motherhood for you. No one has the right to tell you that your motherhood is invalid because your precious baby is no longer in your womb or arms. It is your distinction to acknowledge. The pain is great, but so is the love. You are still a mother. You may not be able to quantify it for others to see, but your lineage indisputably includes the forever, precious babe of your heart and that deserves honor.

ENDURING HOLIDAYS AND MEMORABLE DATES

Those holidays and anniversary dates—horrid, feared, and loathed but somehow survived. Some moms consider such dates for days, weeks, or months ahead. For others, it hides in the subconscious and seemingly slips the mind. Some moms may stare the dates head-on, yet others sustain a sneak attack. One of the most dreaded parts of the day is not knowing how to endure it. Not knowing if you will make it through those twenty-four hours. To face the looming date is a deep reminder the loss occurred. You may relive pregnancy milestones, the events of the day your baby died, or the days in the aftermath of loss. Nevertheless, encountering anniversary dates can be harrowing. Especially, the first dates following the loss, including holidays.

The first Christmas without my boys, I spent the day lying on the edge of the bed in deep sobs. I did not leave the house until that night, hiding from the happiness of others. I was too hurt to see the joy they felt at such a traditionally, cheerful time of family and celebration. On those hard dates, you may want to stop the world and make time for yourself. And that's okay. You may need to leave the city for a day to have solitude or maybe you can opt to stay at home and allow yourself to be still and process your emotions. It's important to resist imposing expectations on yourself or accepting them from others: *I should... What will they think or say if I don't...?* Daily, you are living the best you can and criticizing yourself will only use needed energy to grieve and heal. Remember this: each person is different and what works best for one mom may not work well for you. Give thought to how you can be intentional in making it through the rough days because, as you know, they will come.

Since 2007, I have learned much about myself and my emotional needs in navigating holidays and my sons' birthday. During the first years of loss, I took trips on their birthday, including spending time in the Great Smoky Mountains of Tennessee. I enjoyed those few days of being in a new environment, seeing different sights and sounds. Planning this experience was helpful—a needed option to assist me in managing grief. For their first birthday, I also purchased a cake as many families do to celebrate the milestone. It may seem absurd to some that a mother to angel babies would keep this tradition. Why should it not be an option for an angel parent to honor their baby? Nevertheless, my sons' birthday is celebrated in some form, big or small—taking a day trip, preparing a special dinner, or being quiet and reflecting. The brief life my sons sustained is and will always be honored. Forever a bitter-sweet time, but in recent years I smile much more on those days even if tears are present.

My prayer for you is that you will be empowered in grieving, knowing that you have rights on how you choose to manage your hurt and pain daily and especially on particular dates. Time will move forward at the same pace each day and we cannot reset the clock. We cannot undo the greatest hurt imaginable in losing our babies, but we can make each day and week of growth matter in loss. Yes, there is a hole in your core, an unfillable chasm—that is the reality; however, the truth is that you can in your own time, purpose to make your baby's life matter while enduring difficult dates. Several examples are provided below to help you create a plan in handling those times.

Activities to Honor Your Precious Baby

- **Grow a Garden**. If you have a bona fide green thumb (or not), plant a garden of flowers, fruits, herbs, or vegetables. Gardening is a great way to be active and create a living thing to tend to in honoring your precious angel.

- **Support a Cause**. Since 2008, our family has faithfully supported the March of Dimes' March for Babies. In our pursuit to honor my sons and end premature birth and pregnancy and infant loss, we have raised approximately $20,000 to date. Our local march is usually held during their birthday month in April, which makes it a special time for our family and friends to come together in this way. We walk and raise awareness for the cause so others will not have to sacrifice as we have. This form of advocacy may be a positive outlet for you and your family.

- **Create a Family Tradition**. Make a tradition of lighting a candle on special dates to honor your baby. Create holiday ornaments. Create a daily gratitude journal or jar. Choose a time to review the journal or jar's contents and reflect on what you are grateful for.

- **Take a Trip**. Plan a day trip on an anniversary date or a week-long getaway to honor your angel. A change of environment can be helpful in managing and making meaning in loss.

- **Get a Tattoo**. Create a design that resonates with you and is a tangible expression of your love for and connection to your baby.

- **Wear a Keepsake**. Choose a handmade piece of jewelry or buy a piece each year to remember your child. A lovely beaded necklace or bracelet can be worn daily to honor your little one.

- **Create a Shadowbox**. Frame images associated with your baby, as well as items such as pregnancy test results, ultrasound photos, footprints, gowns, blankets, or a handwritten note.

- **Start a Non-Profit Foundation**. On this grief journey, we realize that our hurt as angel moms is not an anomaly. A foundation is a powerful testament to your baby's lifetime and can also work to provide needed help to others dealing with pregnancy and infant loss. Many organizations are created to satisfy this need. Working with those who support your foundation also creates connection to a common goal and may also provide you support as you work to assist others.

- **Create an Educational Scholarship to Support Youth**. To honor your baby's life and provide an opportunity to pay it forward or benefit a child in need, create a scholarship to support an ambitious youth. As a tribute, you can award this scholarship during your baby's birthday month or other special dates and holidays.

- **Volunteer with a Local Agency**. Serve families in need at a local food pantry or shelter. Adopt a family or child during Christmas, providing items they want or need for the holiday. Taking part in activities to extend your concern to others is a positive means to manage grief and sadness as you transfer your energy to improving someone else's wellbeing.

WRITING A LETTER TO YOUR BELOVED BABY

To ease the emotional aches of holiday and anniversary dates (or honestly, any difficult day), you may receive comfort in writing a letter to your beloved baby. Such dates can cause your mind to linger on thoughts of your precious one. The brief moments you held tiny feet and hands. The heartbeat you heard for the first time. The wonder of the positive pregnancy test. Memories so close but too far away now. The words may be hard to organize at first, but for this exercise, take a breath and let your emotions fill the page. Penning all that you feel but find hard to speak to others, write freely and unhindered to your baby. Use these prompts to guide you in this exploration. I have also included an example.

- *My dearest baby, you mean _____ to me.*

- *I will always treasure our precious time together. I miss _____.*

- *I would have loved to _____.*

- *I will honor and love you by _____.*

My precious Kyle and Kendrick, you are my lovely sons, my princes. The weight of the eternity you've spent away from me physically can't be measured. Though I've never seen your eyes, or heard your softest cries, you're imprinted so deeply in my being. That you once breathed life sustains me and gives purpose to the days lived without you.

_____

_____

_____

_____

SPEAKING YOUR BABY'S NAME

Establishing and using your voice as an angel mom is a crucial piece of defining motherhood. This use of your voice also includes naming and speaking the name of your precious one. Losing a baby can be ignored or overlooked in the face of pain—a hushed, hidden topic even in intimate circles of friends and families. Many people fear mentioning our beloved babies because it is uncomfortable for or even insignificant to them. Why are our babies' lifetimes not important because of their brief duration? Why are our children pitied? Why must they be a phantom in our lives? In our courage to fight stigma and not allow our children to fade into the shadows of our families' histories, we will name our babies and speak their names because we have the right to do so. No matter our babies' ages in gestation. No matter if our babies' genders were determined or not. No matter if birth certificates were issued or not. All life is precious.

You did not expect to complete this assignment, in this way. During pregnancy, when thinking of naming your baby, you might have researched different names and their meanings; made lists of likes and dislikes; rehearsed the sound of the names; or debated with family members on your top choices. Maybe you had not yet started contemplating names. Lovely mom, if you have not named your baby, take time to consider your right to do so. Give yourself permission now—

even if you did not consider this inherent right—and take a stance to honor and declare a name for your baby. A name you esteem and take pride in as you acknowledge your forever bond to your baby and your baby's place in your family. For some people, it may seem odd for a mom to name her angel baby. However, many individuals name possessions of value such as cars or even adored animals and pets, so why don't we have the right to name (and speak the name of) our dear babies?

The day I went into premature labor, before I knew I was having contractions, I recall making a list of potential names, in which Kingston, Kyle, and Kendrick were top contenders. I did not know my boys would soon enter and leave the physical world but the presence and meaning of the names Kyle and Kendrick resonated with me, so they were the winning pair. And now, because of their carefully chosen names, every time I speak my sons' names, I give life to our love, their mark in our family, and their mission. I have so much pride in their bold, regal names that grief and loss does not diminish their identity for me because I use my right—my voice—to speak their names. I say them as often as I can—as any mother would—and I support your right in doing the same.

At this very moment, take a few seconds and speak your baby's/babies' name(s). Inhale and exhale the name. In honor, in sorrow, in love, in longing, speak it. You have the right to acknowledge the precious life you created. You do. And if you are comfortable with others speaking your baby's name, they can and will too.

IN REFLECTING

Ask yourself: *How will I give myself permission to define motherhood? How will I honor my baby and our precious bond?*

_____

_____

_____

_____

IN AFFIRMING

I am still a mother.
Guilt and shame do not define my motherhood.
_____, my love, I will always speak your name.

PART VI

Because our hearts are shaped and tenderized in loss, we can bear witness to our transformation in loss. Bear witness to our testimonies, our motherhood. Your individual sound in sharing your truth is a power you have that grief cannot muffle or stifle. Never underestimate the importance of your declaration. Your baby matters. You matter.

On Transforming in Loss

A PART OF you—at your center—ceases to live with the final beat of your baby's heart. You are forever impacted and profoundly changed. Still, the absence of your baby doesn't invalidate the life you created. In grief and loss, mothers love, mothers protect, mothers nurture, mothers defend, and mothers persevere. Do these words resonate with you? When you think about your beloved baby, do these words define your position? Throughout your grief journey, you may question your role as a mom. The emotions you feel because of the life you don't physically hold can mock motherhood in the face of others. As I explained in "Defining Motherhood," beloved mom, to honor our babies, is to acknowledge ourselves. No, we have not received the gift of reviewing report cards; attending graduations and recitals; or even giving well-deserved spankings and timeouts; however, as angel moms we mother in our own way. As we grow in loss, we are proud to speak about our babies, sharing our loss stories with others. We have individual and family traditions in honoring our babies. So many special ways we treasure them, publicly and privately. Creatively and with intention, we cultivate ways to acknowledge our babies in our present lives. In the absence of and longing for our precious ones, we still love our babies. We remember our babies. We cherish our babies. We are proud of our babies. With every fiber of our literal beings, we are forever connected to our babies.

BEARING WITNESS AND TESTIFYING

Because our hearts are shaped and tenderized in loss, we can bear witness to our transformation in loss. Bear witness to our testimonies, our motherhood. Your individual sound in sharing your truth is a power you have that grief cannot muffle or stifle. Never underestimate the importance of your declaration. Your baby matters. You matter. Your voice in speaking to loss is a legacy for your baby. A great tribute to your child's lifetime.

You may believe that your story is insignificant—even the most disheartening details—but your ability to testify your experience and share with someone on a similar path in grief may be the words they need to hear to maintain a sense of stability and understanding. Dear mom, simply put, if you don't give the testimony, no one will hear or feel it. Resist shrinking and minimizing your voice because you fear that others may not understand, relate to, or agree with your story. Resist muffling your voice because of embarrassment, self-blame, or self-doubt. Your plan for motherhood did not manifest as you hoped and deserved but—with no qualification or quantification needed—you are a mom. Own, express, and acknowledge every aspect of what this path has entailed for you. This is the power and platform you have. Look grief in the eyes and declare you have the right to use your platform as you choose.

Please know it has been a staggering emotional climb for me to get to this point on my grief and healing journey. I have experienced wonderful moments as an angel mom from leading March for Babies walks honoring my sons' lives and other angels and neonatal intensive care unit survivors, to supporting others during their darkest phases in life. I have also sat with the deepest hurt known in burying my greatest loves in a single, tiny casket. Cried tears chorused by sounds I did not know I could produce. I have sat in low moments, ready to die. But love, resilience, will, faith, prayer, and a resolve to honor my sons, propels me beyond grief and loss to move in my pain to serve others. I continue to work on my thoughts and my heart, challenging my fears and even sorrow itself to make it to this point in healing. Still, in my quiet times, when I consider loss and the millions of moments I could have spent with my boys, I can barely breathe thinking about the weight of living without them. I still sob. I still work through feelings of regret, because I still hurt in their absence—and will forever—but then there are moments when I smile, when I recognize the mighty impact my boys continue to make even though they were only on this planet for such a brief time. I smile because our love is greater than loss. It is infinite. Transcending. And as our love deepens, my story in motherhood, my testimony, will change as I grow in loss.

DEFINING YOUR STORY

Dear loss mom, what is your story? As an exercise of reflection, complete the questions below to aid and empower you in defining your story. Our stories in loss transform as we evolve in loss. Your answers to these questions today may vary five weeks, five months, or five years from now as we are constantly stretching and growing in loss. No matter the current coordinates on your grief journey, you have a developing path. Consider this:

- *What has this loss cost me? What have I lost? Emotionally, physically, spiritually, financially, etc.?*

Besides our physical connection with our precious babies, loss takes many things from us, primary and secondary. In losing a baby are present and future losses. For example, the loss of baby showers, maternity photo shoots, and witnessing your child's milestones, are coupled with the loss of innocence and dreams. Journal on the following:

- *What remains post my loss(es)? Who or what remains a constant for me despite this life-changing loss (e.g., love and support of family or friends)?*

- *What strengths have I gained to date on my grief journey? How have I grown in loss? How has loss tested and challenged me?*

- *If I created a public service announcement about pregnancy and infant loss, what would I say? What do I want the masses to know?*

- *Who am I? Who am I becoming? What words would I use to describe myself then, now, and in the future?*

- *What have I learned about myself? About others?*

Please use these questions to assist you in organizing your thoughts about your grief journey. If you can, create your own questions or statements about your story.

_____

_____

_____

_____

We may bury our beloveds ceremonially, but we must not hide or entomb our voices and experiences. Cathartically, releasing and telling our stories may be beneficial as it opens us to strength and light while releasing the heavy burden experienced in grief. Reading these words now, you may believe you will never speak or utter the depths of your experience because it reveals such a deep and tender part of you. Or maybe you shared your candid testimony to silence, instead of supportive words and actions. As loss moms, the right to exercise our voices is inherent and not conditional on others' beliefs, permission, or support. Just as you read these words now, I use my voice in faith and hope it will help the mom standing where I stood and the mom standing where I stand. And you can too. This is your path in healing in loss. The only condition needed for your voice is you. In power, please use it.

IN REFLECTING

Ask yourself: *What is my truth and testimony in motherhood? What is my story? The one I tell myself, and others? The story I would offer to a newcomer in loss?*

_____

_____

_____

_____

IN AFFIRMING

My story matters.
My baby matters.
I will grow in loss—not sorrow.

PART VII

Taking breaths in this unplanned reality is a testament to your strength and ability to press ahead. As mothers in loss, we do not move on without our babies, but yes, we do move forward. You do not have the perfect, storybook motherhood, but you do have a compelling testimony as a mom.

In Moving Forward, Not On

SWEET AND ENDEARING mom, this is not the end of your grief journey. Perhaps it's your genesis, but many days of endurance are ahead. You are farther than you ever thought you could be—seconds, minutes, and days beyond parting with your precious baby, beyond some of the most difficult days you have ever encountered. Taking breaths in this unplanned reality is a testament to your strength and ability to press ahead. As mothers in loss, we do not move on without our babies, but yes, we do move forward.

You do not have the perfect, storybook motherhood, but you do have a compelling testimony as a mom. In strength, you are reading this book now and seeking insight and healing to make meaning of your hurt. My prayer and solemn desire for you is to continue healing on your grief journey and be a positive force for yourself, your family, and others who will, unfortunately, join our tribe. You and I are not alone. But sometimes we suffer alone and that is why your strength—our strength—is vital to support others. Too many women will shed silent tears if we do not use our struggles in loss to heal ourselves and others. Too many women will believe the lie that there is no strength in grieving. Too many loss moms will believe their tears and mourning are signs of weakness, hiding them from self and others.

But not you. Now, equipped with emotional tools to manage grief, you can act assertively and empowered in loss. Defying loss and others' expectations of how you will mother and honor your baby, you will navigate your grief journey. As you work to move forward in taking care of self, also consider how you may join with others impacted by loss such as volunteering with local groups providing services to bereaved mothers, or even offering this book as a resource to facilitate healing can be a powerful gesture in consoling mothers.

A PLEDGE OF HEALING IN LOSS

Throughout this book, you have read affirmations of hope and strength created to encourage and comfort you. As your final exercise in our time together, affirm yourself and create a pledge, in which you craft powerful statements to meditate on and declare. As a guide, I wrote "A Pledge of Healing in Loss" to inspire you.

- *I am a courageous mother to a loved and precious creation.*

- *Loss does not limit my love.*

- *Boldly, I love my baby daily because our connection is infinite.*

- *I grieve and honor my precious one as I choose.*

- *I define my path of healing in grieving.*

- *My journey in loss is unique and valid.*

- *My loss does not have to fit a specific mold or model others' losses.*

- *I will never let my baby's lifetime or our bond be dismissed or forgotten.*

- *I move forward and adapt to loss daily.*

- *I take care of myself—mind, body, and spirit—to endure this journey.*

- *I am kind to and patient with myself.*

- *I will always remember and support the many moms and families who have faced (or will face) pregnancy and infant loss.*

- *I will always remember our babies.*

- *I speak my baby's name.*

- *I treasure the gift of my baby's lifetime.*

- *I am forever a mom.*

Now, it's your turn. With courage and intent, what do you affirm? Write it, speak it, and believe it. Use this pledge daily to focus your thoughts and encourage yourself as you confirm your love in loss.

_____

_____

_____

_____

It has been my honor to support and share with you what I desperately needed in 2007. On this mission to serve, I didn't know how I would reach you, but I knew I needed to get these words to you. I knew I needed to tell you that your baby matters. Your voice and your experiences matter. For all that you have endured. For all that you have seen that you can never un-see. For all that you have lost and given unselfishly, your motherhood matters. Please know the solace you can provide someone who stands by your side or stands now where you stood in loss is immeasurable.

I hope you believe you will move forward. Know that not all associations with your baby will be full of heavy and saddening emotions. You have been so courageous to make it to this point. Please continue to use the tools learned in this exploration. Come back often, reviewing the chapters as needed while transforming and evolving in grief and loss, as this is a lifelong journey now. Take heart, dear mom, you are stronger than you've ever known. Braver than you should've ever been tasked to be. More compassionate than most will ever be. Because of the life you created, you are forever a mother with a loving and deep heart.

Affirmations at a Glance

I have the right to grieve.
In courage, I grieve.
I grieve because I love.
I am capable.
Today, I will practice being still.
I will care for myself by _____.
My grief journey is unique.
I will take a step on my grief journey to _____.
I am healing despite the pain.
I will smile again.
I will honor my grief journey by _____.
Today, I will extend grace to myself.
I am loved.
I will bear each step on my grief journey.
My love for my baby is infinite.
I will grow in loss—not sorrow.
Today, I choose to forgive _____.
Today, I am grateful for _____.
Guilt and shame do not define my motherhood.
_____, my love, I will always speak your name.

I forgive myself and others daily.
I am resilient.
My grief journey is not in vain.
I will not die in this hurt.
I am still a mother.
I choose to believe again despite loss.
My baby matters.
My grief matters.
My story matters.
Grief will not defy my love.

Endnotes

Introduction
1. "Pregnancy and Infant Loss." 2017. The TEARS Foundation. Accessed March 31, 2019. http://thetearsfoundation.org/our-cause/.

Acknowledgements

THIS WORK WOULD not be realized without God and the reassurance of my beloved family and friends. My foundations for life. My greatest motivators and encouragers. The ones who taught me to believe in God first and the talents and abilities He has graciously given me. The ones who instilled a lasting mantra of "Think and Do" in my being, which has afforded me two of my greatest gifts—to write relentlessly, and to believe in God's power within me. I love you all infinitely. I share this moment with you.

On my grief journey, I have met and worked with numerous moms who have also held their precious babies in their wombs and arms for a short time but forever in their hearts. I have gained great strength and connection from this collective of valiant women. Please know you inspire and motivate me to continue in advocating for our cause. Locked hand-in-hand and shoulder-to-shoulder, I support you as you support me. We are forever purposed on this path in honoring our babies, as well as removing shame and stigma in motherhood. I share this moment with you.

For every generous supporter who has given their time,

energy, and funds to the Wells and Hardy families in honoring Kyle and Kendrick at the annual March for Babies, please know you have made a positive, life-changing impact on countless families and future generations. I share this moment with you.

Resources

THIS LISTING FEATURES organizations committed to supporting families surviving pregnancy and infant loss. These groups provide various resources to assist families as they navigate their grief journeys. I hope you will find additional support on this path from a larger community of individuals striving to make meaning in loss. This is not an exhaustive list, so please take time to find resources catered to your specific needs and wants. This list is for information only. I do not endorse or ensure the quality of services provided by these organizations.

Black Angel Mom
www.blackangelmom.com

First Candle
www.firstcandle.org

March of Dimes- Share Your Story
share.marchofdimes.org

The Morning
www.themorning.com

Now I Lay Me Down to Sleep
www.nowilaymedowntosleep.org

Pregnancy After Loss
www.pregnancyafterlosssupport.com

Rachel's Gift
www.rachelsgift.org

Return to Zero: H.O.P.E.
www.rtzhope.org

Share Pregnancy and Infant Loss Support
www.nationalshare.org

Sisters in Loss
www.sistersinloss.com

Star Legacy Foundation
www.starlegacyfoundation.org

Still Birthday
www.stillbirthday.com

Still Standing Magazine
www.stillstandingmag.com

Sunshine After the Storm
www.sunshineafterstorm.us

The TEARS Foundation
www.thetearsfoundation.org

About the Author

KEISHA M. WELLS is a licensed professional counselor and mother to twin angels, Kyle and Kendrick. Keisha's entry into motherhood includes a traumatic, second-trimester loss of multiples. Her sons were born prematurely in 2007 and transitioned shortly after a few hours of precious life. To date, they are her greatest creation.

Keisha is the founder of Transformation Counseling Services, a practice specializing in grief counseling and mental health services for women impacted by pregnancy and infant loss; postpartum depression and anxiety; and traumatic birth experiences. With a call to serve and support others during their most heartbreaking trials in womanhood and motherhood, Keisha practices in Georgia as a compassionate therapist and advocate for underserved populations.

As a perinatal mental health specialist, Keisha's work also includes eradicating injustices in pregnancy and birth experiences via educating women on their rights and assisting them in advocating for their emotional and physical health while working with medical professionals to prevent infant and maternal mortality.

Keisha is an avid reader and writer, contributing to articles in ESSENCE Magazine, The New York Times, Therapy for Black Girls, Bustle, and HuffPost. For more information and to connect with Keisha, visit www.keishawells.com.

www.ingramcontent.com/pod-product-compliance
Lightning Source LLC
Chambersburg PA
CBHW031118080526
44587CB00011B/1017